Hawaiian
Alphabet

a, e, h, i, k, l, m, n, o, p, u, w

Lori Phillips, Ed.D.

PREL

Published by Pacific Resources for Education and Learning (PREL)

900 Fort Street Mall, Suite 1300 • Honolulu, Hawaiʻi 96813
Toll free: (1-800) 377-4773 • Phone: (808) 441-1300 • Fax: (808) 441-1385
Email: askprel@prel.org • Website: www.prel.org

Distributed by Bess Press

3565 Harding Avenue • Honolulu, Hawaiʻi 96816
Toll free: (1-800) 910-2377 • Phone: (808) 734-7159 • Fax: (808) 732-3627
Email: info@besspress.com • Website: www.besspress.com

Cover design by Carol Colbath

Copyright © 2004 by PREL
Second printing 2008

Library of Congress Cataloging-in-Publication Data

Hawaiian alphabet / Lori Phillips.
    p. cm.
    Includes illustrations.
    ISBN 1-57306-218-9
    ISBN 978-1-57306-218-3
    1. Hawaiian language - Alphabet -
Juvenile literature. I. Pacific Resources
for Education and Learning. II. Title.
PL6443.P32 2004   499.4-dc21

Printed in Korea

This product was funded by the U.S. Department of Education (U.S.
ED) under the Regional Educational Laboratory program, award
number ED01CO0014. The content does not necessarily reflect the
views of the U.S. ED or any other agency of the U.S. government.

This book is part of the *Island Alphabet Books* series, which features languages and children's artwork from the U.S.-affiliated Pacific. Each book contains the complete alphabet for the language, four or five examples for each letter, and a word list with English translations. The series is published by PREL, a non-profit corporation that works collaboratively with school systems to enhance education across the Pacific.

Special thanks to the following people and organizations
for their patience and enthusiastic support of this project:
Palama Settlement ICT Learning Center
National Endowment for the Arts
Tom Barlow, Karen Ehrhorn, Kay Fukuda, Nancy Lane, Lee Noto,
Mary Dodd Pearson, and Ludwig David van Broekhuizen
of Pacific Resources for Educational and Learning (PREL)
Celina Shetana and John Sullivan of Digital Majic

This alphabet book has been reviewed by:

Puanani Wilhelm, Administrator
Hawaiian Studies and Language Programs
Hawai'i Department of Education

Keoni K. Inciong, Educational Specialist
Hawaiian Language Immersion Program
Hawai'i Department of Education

Miki Cachola-Solomon
Pacific Resources for Education and Learning

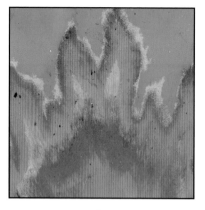

ahi

ao

'awapuhi

'ailana

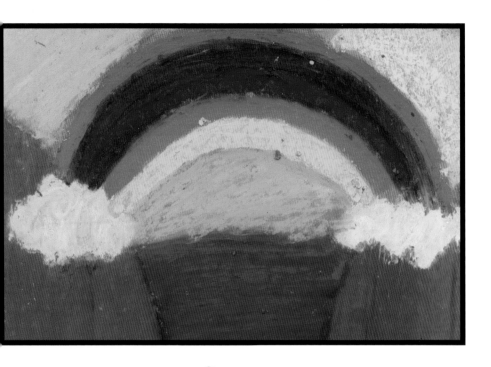

Aa

ānuenue

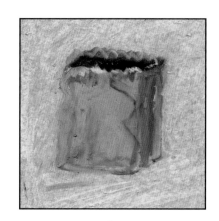

'eke

'elepani

Ee

ʻelelū

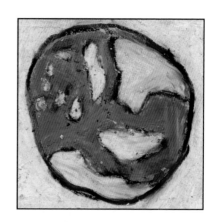

he'e

honua

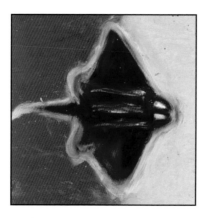

hihimanu

heleuma

Hh

honu

ihu

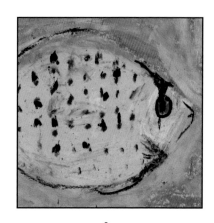

i'a

ipu

Ii

'Īlio

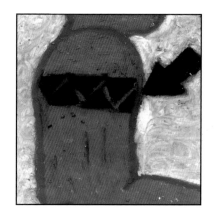

kākau

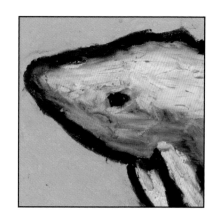

koholā

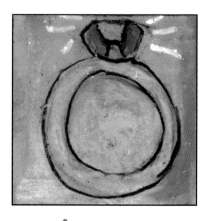

komo

kalo

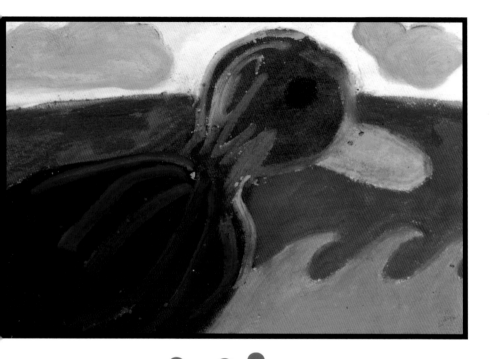

Kk

kakā

lio

lā

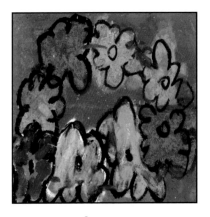

lei

Ll

lua pele

mo'o

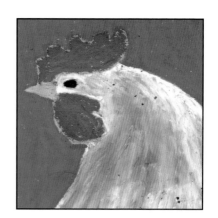

moa

makika

mahina

Mm

mai'a

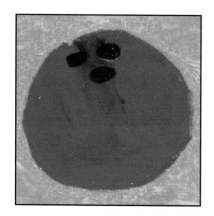

niu

nalo

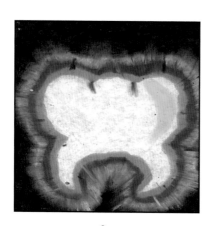

niho

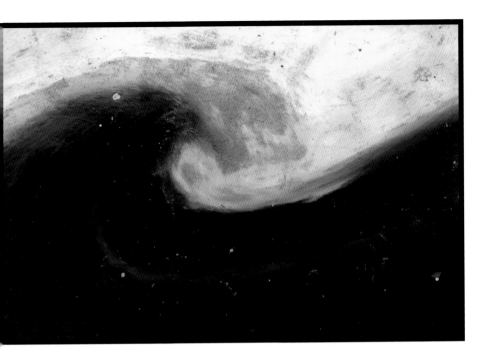

Nn

nalu

'ōpae

oho

'ōpū

Oo

ʻōpeʻapeʻa

pua

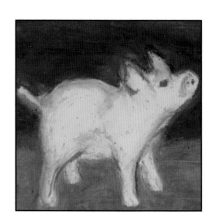

pua'a

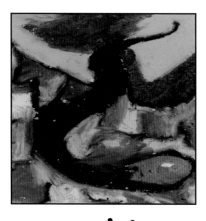

puhi

pāpale

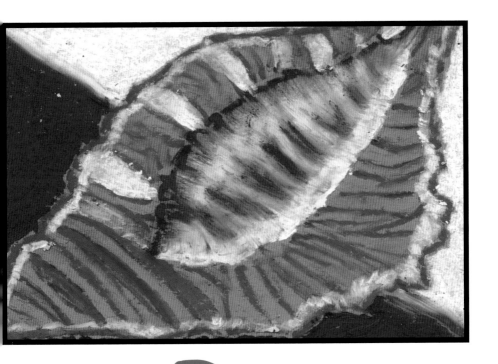

Pp

pūpū

ʻukulele

uapo

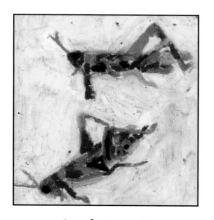

ʻūhini

Uu

'ulu

wai

wana

wahī

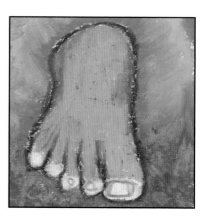

wāwae

Ww

wa'a

English Translations

ahi	fire
'ailana	island
ānuenue	rainbow
ao	clouds
'awapuhi	ginger
'eke	sack
'elelū	cockroach
'elepani	elephant
he'e	octopus
heleuma	anchor
hihimanu	stingray
honu	turtle
honua	world
i'a	fish
ihu	nose
'īlio	dog
ipu	gourd
kakā	duck
kākau	tattoo
kalo	taro

koholā	whale
komo	ring
lā	sun
lei	garland
lio	horse
lua pele	volcano
mahina	moon
maiʻa	banana
makika	mosquito
moa	rooster
moʻo	gecko
nalo	housefly
nalu	wave
niho	tooth
niu	coconut
oho	hair
ʻōpae	shrimp
ʻōpeʻapeʻa	bat
ʻōpū	stomach
pāpale	hat
pua	flower
puaʻa	pig

puhi	eel
pūpū	shell
uapo	dock
'ūhini	grasshopper
'ukulele	ukulele
'ulu	breadfruit
wa'a	canoe
wahī	letter
wai	drink
wana	sea urchin
wāwae	foot

Also available in:

Palauan

Kosraean

Chuukese

Marshallese

Samoan

Pohnpeian

Chamorro

English

Carolinian

Satawalese

Yapese

Woleaian

Ulithian